Native Harvest

Authentic Southwestern Gardening
by Kevin Dahl

Western National Parks Association
Tucson, Arizona

Contents

▲ Fresh corn and
green chiles

▶ Native dent corn

Native
Harvest

▲ *Black sunflower seeds*

Authentic Southwestern Gardening

Your vegetable garden, whether it happens to be in the Southwest or not, can benefit from the centuries-old agricultural legacy of this region. Despite grueling heat, nutrient-poor soils, scarce water, and cunning pests, Native farmers grew enough food to support thriving communities. Over the years they developed vigorous crop varieties and techniques, knowledge, skills, and traditions needed to coax fields of corn, beans, squash, and other vegetables to grow in almost impossible conditions.

In this arid country, Native farmers developed a number of water-wise ways to ensure a successful harvest. Along the major rivers in central  Arizona, canals and irrigation ditches brought water to the fields after spring snowmelt raised the river level, ushering in the first warm-weather crop. Later, during the summer rains, the canals and ditches brought a second growing season to the people living in places such as Central Arizona. Elsewhere in the Sonoran Desert, farmers planted fields at the mouths of foothill washes so that seasonal water flows could irrigate their plots. Zuni farmers grew plants close to their village in gardens that were sculpted with waffle-like indentations, making it easier to water the plants with pitchers of creek water. Most Hopi corn fields look like sand dunes. Beneath the sandy topsoil, layers of clay soil retain snowmelt that nourishes plants during the summer growing season.

Songs, ceremonies, close attention, and hard work accompanied all aspects of Native farming. Trading seeds and stories, farmers adapted plants over time to help them feed their families under a variety of conditions. They also cultivated crops for use as containers, rattles, and utensils (gourds), basket-making material (devil's claws), and fiber (cotton), as well as cooking and medicinal herbs.

> **In the last few decades, Indian farmers from southwestern tribes have shared their knowledge and seeds with others so this tradition can continue.**

Fortunately, traditional southwestern gardening is a living heritage. Though not nearly as widespread as they once were, gardens planted by American Indian farmers are tended and harvested annually. O'odham farmers grow *huuñ* (a short corn that fully matures in 60 days) and *bav* (protein-rich tepary beans) using the summer thunderstorm runoff that reaches their fields in southwestern Arizona. Hopi farmers tend their spring-fed garden terraces below the high mesas where they live in northern Arizona. Like their ancestors centuries ago, Santa Clara Pueblo farmers in present-day New Mexico clear out irrigation ditches so that Río Grande water can support fields of corn. The sprawling Navajo nation—the largest Indian land in our country—has both commercial tribal farms and small plots tended by individual families.

In the last few decades, Indian farmers from southwestern tribes have shared their knowledge and seeds with others so that this tradition can continue. Largely through the work of the nonprofit group Native Seeds/SEARCH, southwestern native seeds have been distributed worldwide and found fertile ground in diverse places. (See page 62 for more information about Native Seeds/SEARCH.) Tohono O'odham *huuñ*, for instance, was the single most productive corn grown by a Norwegian researcher in the short growing season north of the Arctic Circle, while *bav* generates outstanding yields in the driest parts of Africa and Australia. Hopi Blue Corn astounds gardeners throughout North America with large, vibrant plants.

We invite you to plant a native crop garden or to add one or more of these plants to your vegetable garden. This book describes the major southwestern crops and how to grow them—wherever your garden grows.

▼ *Summer harvest*

▲ Several varieties of native corn

▼ Corn silk

Blue corn ▼
seeds

Corn

Corn was the most important traditional southwestern crop—it produced abundant harvests that were easily stored for times of famine. Today many think of "Indian corn" as a colorful Thanksgiving decoration, and some are surprised to learn that it is edible. The beautiful colors reflect the diversity of corn types and different delicious ways to prepare them. For home gardeners looking to try something different, these varieties offer an array of choices.

Corn is categorized into five types based on the starch and sugar content of the kernel: popcorn, sweet, dent, flint, and flour. Native farmers usually grew several varieties of corn, each traditionally used in a unique way. Popcorn is one of the oldest types of domesticated corn. Archeologists dated an ear found in southern New Mexico to 4,500 years ago. Sweet corn, the type with the highest sugar content, is commonly eaten as corn on the cob, either boiled in water or roasted in the husk. Dent corn (named for the dent formed in the dried kernel) and flint corn dry into particularly hard kernels, a quality that affords them better protection against pests.

The type of corn most commonly grown in the Southwest is flour corn, which can be easily ground into a meal. Native people make a delicious snack with the kernels of one type of flour corn by parching them in hot sand, sifting, and then lightly coating the kernels with saltwater. Cooks use ground blue cornmeal for baked goods, stews, stuffings, dumplings, and beverages. One large-kernel variety of white flour corn makes hominy, which in the Southwest and Mexico is used in tamales or a soup called posole.

While corn contains useful amounts of the vitamin niacin, it is in a bound form that is not nutritionally available without preparation. Priming the corn with an alkalinizing agent such as wood ashes or crushed limestone—which is how hominy is made—releases the niacin so that humans can absorb it. Somehow the ancient cooks knew the importance of this procedure. Unfortunately, this knowledge was slow in coming to the Europeans of the 1700s and the southern U.S. farmers of the 1900s. Both groups, who relied on corn (as opposed to hominy) as a primary food, suffered from the niacin-deficiency disease called pellagra.

Corn is a fast-growing plant with a surprisingly small root structure. It does best in loose, fertile soils and requires regular watering (or good rains). Some gardeners add compost, aged manure, or fish emulsion during the growing season to help provide extra nitrogen. High winds can blow corn plants over; if they don't spring back on their own, you can push them up and pack soil around the base. Hopi farmers propped flat

▲ *Blue corn seed*

rocks upwind from young corn plants to
shield them from the wind.

Corn is best planted in
blocks rather than rows to
ensure the full pollination that
results in ears well packed with
plump kernels. Most home
gardeners usually plant only one
type of corn per season because
wind-borne pollen will readily cause
varieties to cross with each other. Growing
native varieties within 100 feet of each other can
cause cross-pollination, turning sweet corn starchy.

Harvest corn depending on when and how
you intend to use it. The best time to harvest sweet corn
for corn on the cob or flour corn for green corn
tamales is when the kernels are in the milk stage.

▲ *Blue cornmeal*

To determine this, select an ear with silks that have turned brown but
are not completely dry. Gently peel back the husk and examine the
kernels. They should not have any color yet and will squirt a milky juice
when pressed with a fingernail. Harvest flour, flint, and dent corns
intended for cornmeal or popcorn after the ears have dried on the stalk.

Southwestern Varieties

Gardeners across the United States have reported success growing
Hopi Blue Corn, a flour type used to make blue cornmeal. This variety
grows vigorously under marginal conditions. Tohono O'odham 60-Day
Corn is an extremely fast-growing white flour corn that produces medium-
sized ears on very short plants. Navajo Copper popcorn is another desert-
adapted small plant that produces beautiful butterscotch-colored ears.

Blue Corn Pancakes

1 cup blue cornmeal*

1 teaspoon salt

1 cup boiling water (or enough to make the mixture "gooey")

1 egg

$1/2$ cup milk

2 tablespoons melted butter

$1/2$ cup sifted whole wheat pastry flour or unbleached white flour[†]

2 teaspoons baking powder

Option: After mixing in the flour, fold in 1 cup fresh or frozen blueberries.

  * May substitute equivalent amount of yellow cornmeal.

  [†] May substitute Pima club wheat flour, roasted or not.

Place the blue cornmeal, salt, and boiling water in a large bowl, stir slowly, then cover and let stand 10 minutes. In a small bowl, beat together the egg, milk, and butter. Add the egg mixture to the cornmeal mixture, then add the flour and baking powder, stirring to blend. Fold in blueberries, if desired. In a very hot skillet (we've found a nonstick skillet works best), pour batter into 4-inch rounds. Flip pancakes when most of the bubbles forming on the surface have burst (about 5 minutes on each side). Makes about 12 cakes.

▲ *Pole beans on trellis*   *Tepary beans* ◀

▼ *Shell beans*

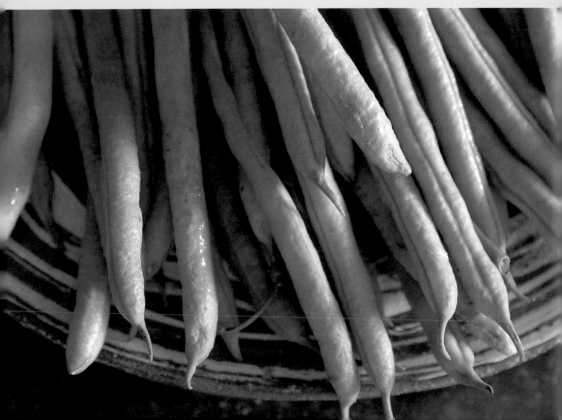

Beans

Planting

Time: After the last frost when soil temperature
      reaches 60°F

Depth: 1/2 to 1 inch

Space between plants: 6 inches

Seed preparation: Use inoculant for more productive
      plants (see below)

Days to maturity: 60 to 100

Tips: Install a trellis when planting to avoid disturbing
      plants after germination

Southwestern beans—a mainstay crop for traditional farmers—are tasty, easy to grow, and nutritious. They come in a rich variety of colors and beautiful markings, with enough magic to make trading a family cow for a handful not such a bad proposition. Low in fat and sodium, high in protein, and with plenty of healthy fiber, vitamins, and minerals, beans are a nearly perfect food. Modern gardeners and cooks are lucky indeed if their plots and pantries are full of beans!

Four bean species comprise this regional diversity: Common beans, *Phaseolus vulgarus*, make up the largest group, including such cultivars as pinto, kidney, pink, white, and string beans. Scarlet runner beans, *Phaseolus coccineus*, have showy flowers and large beans; the plant thrives in the cooler temperatures of the Southwest's higher elevations and can be a perennial in some climates. Lima beans, *Phaseolus lunatus*, are productive in long growing seasons. On the other hand, tepary beans,

Phaseolus acutifolius, are adapted to growing fast in hot summers, much like the wild desert relatives from which they were domesticated. First cultivated in the Southwest by the Hohokam culture, tepary beans mature quickly and thrive despite desert heat, drought, and alkaline soils. They are well adapted to producing a crop with just one or two irrigations, as might occur in Tohono O'odham floodwater fields. Backyard gardeners tend to provide too much water, producing lush, leafy plants with few beans. When mature, the plant continues growing until the summer rains

Beans are very easy to grow.

stop. Holding back water signals to the plant that it is time to set and mature a heavy crop of beans.

Southwestern beans tend to be pole beans rather than bush beans. Pole beans are preferable for home gardens over compact bush beans, which were developed for mechanical harvesting. Pole beans are easier to pick and more productive, may taste better than similar bush varieties, and produce beans over a longer period. Pole beans, as the name implies, require something to support their vines, such as a tipi-like arrangement of poles, trellis, netting, or fencing material.

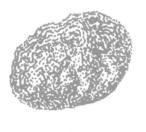

▲ *Tepary bean*

Beans are also divided into three categories—snap, shell, and dry—based on the growth stage when they're usually picked and eaten. Pick snap beans (also called green beans) when the pods are young and tender, before the seeds start swelling, and eat the entire pod either raw or cooked. Harvest shell beans (or shellies) when the pods are plump but before they start turning brown, removing the tender beans from the pod before eating. Collect dry beans from pods that are done growing and have thoroughly dried, usually on the plant. Some southwestern varieties make good snap beans; most can be eaten as shellies or dry beans.

Dry beans ready for cooking ◄

Beans, like most plants in the legume family, host bacteria on their roots that convert atmospheric nitrogen found in soil into forms that plants can use. In nature, the bacteria are plentiful where wild legumes grow, but this is not necessarily the case in garden soil. Many gardeners use an inexpensive inoculant powder that contains these beneficial bacteria; it is available from seed catalogs and nurseries. Dust or lightly coat bean seeds with moistened inoculant just before planting. Inoculated plants grow bigger and produce more beans.

Beans are very easy to grow. Their roots don't like to be disturbed, so plant them directly in the garden and set up poles or trellises before the seedlings emerge. Beans are prone to viruses and other diseases that can be prevented by simple practices: rotating crops, planting in full sun in well-drained soil, keeping the garden weed free, and watering carefully to keep the plants dry. Water in the early morning and provide the water at ground level. After a rain, avoid working among the plants until they have dried. Should a plant appear diseased (stunted growth, curling or puckering of leaves, or mottling on leaves), remove and discard the entire plant.

Beans are mostly self-pollinating, so different cultivars within the same species can be grown side by side with little cross-pollination. (Plant 10 feet apart to completely avoid crossing.)

Southwestern Varieties

White Teparies are sweeter than Brown Teparies, which have a nuttier taste. Anasazi Beans, though not productive in very hot climates, produce a sweet, fast-cooking, colorful dry bean that is reputed to cause less intestinal gas than other types. Hopi Purple String Beans make delicious snap beans and beautiful dry beans, purple with black crescent moon–shaped stripes. Four Corners (deep purple and black beans) or Aztec (white) Runner Beans both have beautiful bright red flowers and delicious large beans that soak up the flavor of added spices. Hopi Orange Limas produce an abundance of brilliant orange-and-red mottled beans.

Bean Soup

1 pint frijoles (pinto beans or any other
dry bean; very good with Tohono O'odham
Pink beans)

2 quarts cold water

1/2 tablespoon salt

1 sliced onion

1 chile pulp or 1 1/2 teaspoons chile powder

2 cloves garlic

1 tablespoon Mexican oregano

Wash beans well and soak overnight. Boil very slowly. When beans are half done, add salt.
When tender, add onion, chile, garlic, and oregano. Simmer until all are tender. Add water
until soup is the desired consistency.

Scarlet Runner Beans and Squash

1 pound Four Corners Scarlet Runner Beans
          (a Navajo variety)*

7 cloves garlic, chopped or pressed

1 medium onion

2 carrots, chopped

1 cup Navajo Hubbard (or any other winter squash), rind removed and cubed

10 cups of water or broth (meat or vegetable)

salt as desired

*The scarlet runner bean's large size and the way it soaks up flavors makes this dish special.
But if unavailable, you can substitute your favorite dry bean.

Place all ingredients except for salt in a crockpot set to high. Cook for 1 hour on high, then
reduce heat to low and cook for an additional 8 hours or until beans are tender. When beans
are softened, add desired salt. Serves 6 to 8.

▲ *Squash blossom*

▼ *Squash*

Tohono O'odham ◄
squash seed

Squash

Squash—a category of plant that includes pumpkins—can truly take over your garden during the growing season and your kitchen and pantry at harvest time. A mainstay of southwestern farming traditions, it pays many dividends for the home gardener.

Squash produced two crops, and several types of food, for the Native farmer. Gardeners harvested some of the small, soft-skinned, immature fruit to prepare as "summer squash." They left the rest of the fruit to grow into large "winter squash," which produces plentiful, sweet flesh. The southwestern varieties have tough rinds and can keep for several months without refrigeration. Some Native farmers stored squash in piles covered with cornstalks, while others kept them in specially constructed storehouses built of arrowweed, willow, and cornstalks. Farmers cut squash flesh into long strips or chips and dried them in the sun like beef jerky. The dried flesh could be stored almost indefinitely. Roasted squash seeds also stored well, though because the seeds made such a delicious snack, they were not likely to last long! Some Native cooks ground squash seeds with other oilseeds, condiments, and fruit to make a sauce, mole pipiáen, which is served today in Mexican cuisine.

The beautiful, large squash flowers are also a delicious vegetable. Gardeners collect male blossoms in particular, which they might fry with other vegetables or add to soups and stews. Male flowers tend to appear first, toward the end of the vines; female ones are more common in the center of the plant and have an unmistakable small bulb at their base that, if fertilized, will grow into a squash. You can ensure a bumper crop by hand-pollinating your squash flowers, transferring pollen from male to female flowers. Some people use a small artist's brush for this; others pull off male flowers and shake the pollen into the female blossoms.

> **A healthy crop of flowering plants and herbs nearby will encourage beneficial insects that eat aphids and beetles.**

Fast-growing squash vines can crowd out other plants in your vegetable patch. Where space is limited, place squash on the garden's edge and train vines into otherwise unproductive yard areas. Successful squash gardeners plan for prolific growth by enriching the soil before planting with plenty of compost or composted manure. Monthly applications of a nitrogen-rich fertilizer (for example, fish emulsion or side dressings of manure) can be helpful throughout the growing season.

Squash plants need regular deep irrigations (down to 24 inches) to maintain growth, but once fruit has set, it is best to water judiciously to prevent fungus. Contact with damp soil can cause maturing fruit to mold, a problem Native farmers solved by putting weeds or stones underneath each squash fruit. Squash leaves will indicate when the plant needs water: to prevent water loss during hot days, squash leaves go limp. If they are still limp the next morning, the plant should be watered. Harvest your winter squash by cutting the vine—don't pull—at least an inch from the fruit. The dried bit of vine makes a great carry handle later on.

Pests can be troublesome throughout the squash life cycle. Birds find the seedlings tasty and also will dig up recently planted seeds. Protect them with chicken wire or upside-down plastic berry baskets. A healthy crop of flowering plants and herbs nearby will encourage beneficial insects that eat aphids and beetles which attack squash plants; a good hosing (for aphids) and picking off by hand (for beetles) are simple pest-fighting strategies.

Squash seed ▲

Southwestern Varieties

Squash comes in different sizes, shapes, colors, and flavors. Tohono O'odham Ha:l is a heat-tolerant, short-season, green-and-white-striped squash that is prized for both its immature fruit (called *ha:l mamat*, or squash children, by the O'odham) and the light orange flesh of the fully grown fruit. Magdalena Big Cheese looks like a flattened pumpkin with a dusky orange skin (like an old-fashioned wheel of cheese); its bright orange flesh is sweet. Mayo Blusher's white and sometimes light-green fruits are elongated and "blush" pink when the sweet, apricot-colored flesh is fully ripe.

Sipongviki
(Hopi Baked Squash Blossoms)

12 large squash blossoms

1 cup blue cornmeal

1/2 teaspoon salt

3 tablespoons bacon drippings
(or vegetable shortening or oil)

3/4 cup water (approximately)

green chiles (optional)

Early in the morning, before the blossoms close, cut blossoms with a sharp knife. Rinse the blossoms gently and drain. Mix cornmeal, salt, and shortening in a mixing bowl. Slowly add water, while stirring, to make thick dough that you can handle with your fingers. Gently stuff the blossoms with a teaspoon of dough each. Fold blossom edges over the dough, to keep dough from falling out while baking. Place blossoms stem up on a lightly greased cookie sheet. Bake in a 300°F oven for 20 minutes. You may add chopped green chiles to the dough.

▲ *Row of amaranth covered to prohibit cross-pollination*　　　*Amaranth seeds* ▲

▼ *Amaranth bloom*

Would you like to grow candy in your garden? Amaranth seeds, popped and mixed with honey, make a confection called *alegría* (happy) found in Mexican supermarkets or sold by street vendors in that country's major cities.

Amaranth varieties have been grown for both food and ornament the world over. Flower enthusiasts are well acquainted with Cockscomb, Love-Lies-Bleeding, Prince's Feather, Globe Amaranth, and Celosia. All make long-lasting cut and dried flowers of various colors and forms. The plant's name comes from the Greek word for unwithering, in reference to the long-lived blossoms, which have symbolized immortality through the ages.

While eating amaranth won't bring immortality, it certainly adds to a healthy diet. The cooked green leaves are rich in iron, calcium, niacin, vitamin C, and vitamin A, comparing well to the nutrition in spinach. The seeds and the flour made from them are also packed with vitamins and minerals, and are

Planting

Time: After the last frost, when soil temperature is 65°F

Depth: 1/2 to 1/8 inch, or broadcast and rake in

Space between plants: Thin to 1 foot apart

Seed preparation: None required

Days to maturity: 100 to 130

Tips: Save the seedlings you thin to add to a salad

Amaranth

a good source of protein. A single cup of the cooked grain provides 28 grams of protein—more than half of an adult's daily requirement.

For the Aztecs of Mexico, protein-rich amaranth was a major crop, as important to their economy and rituals as corn. Ceremonial amaranth cakes

Protein-rich amaranth was a major crop for the Aztecs of Mexico

were formed into the shapes of gods and were sometimes made with human blood from sacrificial victims. Repulsed by the ritual use of this plant, the Spanish banned its growth and consumption.

In the far northern reaches of New Spain, Native farmers continued to grow the domesticated amaranth that had been introduced via trade with their southern neighbors. Amaranth was never as important a crop in the Southwest as in Mexico. Not all Native groups grew it, in fact. But most were acquainted with a wild amaranth that still shows up as a weed in gardens and fields. Called pigweed or careless weed, it was tolerated by many farmers who gathered the young plants to cook. Today, O'odham families still enjoy "Indian spinach" made with amaranth and a few other wild greens.

Gardeners will discover that domesticated varieties of amaranths grow as quickly and easily as any weed, making them easy for kids to grow. They require full sun and only occasional watering. Plant them where you won't mind large, tall plants. Disease and pests are seldom a problem. When the flowers start to dry and produce seed, or after the first hard frost, tie a paper grocery sack around the large seed head. Cut the thick stem below and let the head dry further in the bag. Many seeds will fall onto the bottom of the bag, and others can be separated from other plant material by rubbing. Winnow off the chaff. It is inevitable that some seed will have fallen off the plant earlier and will likely produce amaranth plants in your garden next year.

Amaranth seed can be cooked whole as a hot cereal or ground finely in a mill or blender to produce gluten-free flour. A minor but upcoming alternative crop for American farmers, amaranth has entered the health-food market in breakfast cereals, pastas, cookies, breads, and the like. In baking, you can replace the amount of flour called for in a recipe with one part amaranth flour to three or four parts wheat flour. Home producers can also pop the seeds in a hot-air popper or in an ungreased steel wok or cast-iron skillet over medium heat. Use one tablespoon of seeds and keep them moving with a brush or spoon to prevent burning. If the seeds don't pop well, sprinkle the next batch lightly with water and try later when they've had time to absorb the moisture.

Southwestern Varieties

Chefs love to enhance salads with the burgundy red seedlings and tender young leaves of Hopi Red Dye Amaranth, a plant the Hopi traditionally used to add red color to wafer-thin *piki* (cornbread). Mano de Obispo, "Bishop's Hand," has golden and magenta flowers that, along with marigolds, decorate graves for Día de los Muertos, All Souls Day, on November 2. Alegríea or Mexican Grain will produce an abundance of delicious seeds of the type used in Mexican candy.

▲ Red chiles

▼ Green chiles

Santo Domingo ▼
Chile seeds

Chiles

After the tomato, the pepper is the most popular plant in American vegetable gardens—perhaps because there are so many wonderful varieties from which to choose, from sweet bell peppers to fiery jalapeños. It wasn't always so in the Southwest. Before the Spanish brought domesticated chile varieties north from Mexico, only a few tribal groups collected or traded for a small but tasty wild chile found along the U.S.-Mexico border. Today, chiles are an integral part of traditional southwestern gardening and cuisine. Indeed, long strings of drying red chile pods, called *ristras*, are an enduring image of this region.

It's said that *ristras* hanging by the front door once signified a farmer's good harvest and that there would be food to share with hungry travelers. Modern visitors to the chile-growing regions can buy *ristras*—and other chile products—at roadside stands and specialty shops.

In some parts of the Southwest, the wild chile is still a cherished spice. Wild-harvested in northern Mexico, the hot, pea-sized chiltepin adds a distinctive flavor to many restaurant salsas. In other restaurants, a shaker of dried chiltepines is available to those who ask. Birds steal the fruit from Mexican American and other heat-loving family gardens, spreading the seeds far and wide, so that new plants show up unbidden and unrecognized in Tucson and Phoenix yards.

Many birds love chiles, much to a gardener's chagrin. For them, it's an arrangement of mutual benefit. Chiles provide carbohydrates, a

▲ Wild chiltepin seed

little protein, and lots of vitamins (and for some birds, such as cardinals, the chemistry that helps make their feathers red). In turn, a bird's digestive system prepares the seed for planting, packages it with water and fertilizer, and drops it under a tree (where these chiles like to grow). In general, chiles don't like mammals to interrupt this cycle—our grinding teeth and longer digestive systems are bad for the seeds. The heat in chiles, caused by a chemical called capsaicin, isn't felt by birds but registers hot and painful for other animals. In fact, humans are the only mammal that regularly eats chiles. Many of us have learned to love the pain!

Eat chile peppers fresh when immature (green) or when ripened to their mature color (which is often red, but can be yellow, orange, brown, purple, or black). Chile peppers also can be dried, pickled, canned, frozen, or smoked. Dried peppers are crushed (as are the Italian chile flakes found on every pizzeria table) or powdered. Different varieties have distinctive flavors, and come in fruits as small as 1/2 inch or as long as 12 inches. They can have no heat at all or be almost too hot to eat, with an abundance of capsaicin.

Capsaicin is located in the placental tissue of the chile fruit, near the seeds. That's why removing the seeds (and the tissue along with them) will tone down the temperature of some chiles. Take care when harvesting and preparing hot chiles; capsaicin in the eyes, on other soft tissues, or even on the skin can feel very unpleasant. Wear gloves and use caution. Should you or a friend eat a chile that proves too hot, water won't help.

For "chile first aid" milk, bread, tortilla chips, or something else with a little oil in it will do a better job.

Chiles grow a lot like tomatoes. Most gardeners start them from seed indoors or purchase seedlings at a nursery. In climates with a long hot growing season, plant seeds directly in the garden 1 inch apart and thin later to proper spacing.

Seeds need warm soil temperatures to germinate, ideally 85°F. To get pepper plants started indoors, use a sterile potting mixture to avoid virus problems. Keep seedlings warm and moist, using bottled water if possible (or let tap water stand overnight to remove any traces of chlorine). Once the seedlings have sprouted, provide a source of sunlight or a growing lamp and weekly feedings of a mild liquid fertilizer. A week or two before planting, seedlings should be "hardened off," which means placing them outside in a sheltered place for a few hours, leaving them a little longer each day so that they will get used to outdoor conditions.

Transplant the healthy seedlings to garden beds after all danger of frost is past and the soil temperature is at least 65°F. Do this in the early evening or on a cloudy day, and water immediately, to help avoid transplant shock. Place the plants 1 inch lower in the ground than they grew in their pots to encourage additional root growth.

Chile pepper plants are easy to grow, with few pest problems.

Chile pepper plants are easy to grow, with few pest problems. People who use tobacco should wash their hands with soap and water before handling pepper plants to prevent the spread of tobacco mosaic disease. Proper watering, to keep the soil uniformly moist but not soggy, can prevent other problems. Underwatering a crop can cause blossoms to shed, peppers to grow smaller, and a dry rot called blossom-end rot to form on the tips of peppers. Overwatering can result in Phytophthora root rot, causing the plant to wilt and die suddenly. Use mulch—such as straw, grass clippings, or plastic—to keep moisture even and reduce weeds. Varieties with large fruits (bell peppers, for instance) will benefit from sturdy support from a small tomato cage or similar device.

Beautiful chile pepper plants can be included in an ornamental bed or enjoyed in a decorative container. The ideal size of container for a pepper plant is 5 gallons or larger, though smaller is okay if the purpose is to overwinter a plant that will be returned to the garden come spring. In no-frost areas, or in properly cared-for containers, chiles can be the perennial plants they are in their natural habitat.

Southwestern Varieties

How do you choose among the hundreds of chile varieties available? When you mull over what to try, consider one or two of these southwestern favorites. Chile del árbol (tree chile) has long, thin pods that are used to make a hot salsa. Chimayo chilés are similar to the longtime native New Mexican chiles: mild, good-tasting, and early maturing. Larger-fruited Anaheim chiles are good for stuffing (chile rellenos), canning, freezing, or drying. Eat thick-fleshed jalapeños fresh, pickled, and in jellies—or smoked to create a delicious dried chile called chipotle.

Roasted Fresh Green Chiles

Select enough fresh green chiles to serve your family—at least one per person. Wash chiles and allow to dry; or wipe them dry with a paper towel. Place in a shallow pan and roast in a 400°F oven, turning them so that all sides become blistered. Steam the blistered chiles by placing a wet cloth on top of the pan for 10 to 15 minutes, or until the skin loosens and can be peeled easily. When cool enough to handle, roll the chiles gently between the hands, further loosening the skins, then peel. The peeled chiles may be frozen or canned for use at a later date. Or they can be chopped or pureed in a blender.

Green chiles can be blistered over charcoal as well as on a stove or in an oven, but they must be turned often—no matter where they are roasted—to prevent burning. They add interest to any dish. Hopi cooks frequently serve them as a topping for eggs, as a spread for sandwiches, or in stews.

▲ Devil's claw dried seed pods

Devil's claw seed ▼

▼ Devil's claw plants with growing seedpods

Planting

Time: After the last frost, when soil temperature is 75°F

Depth: 1/2 inch

Space between plants: 3 feet

Seed preparation: Presoak, scarify, or completely
     remove the seed coat to reveal the kernel

Days to maturity: 60

Tips: Keep soil moist until seedlings germinate

Devil's Claw

Southwestern Native baskets, highly prized today for their beauty and workmanship, were traditionally used every day for storing or carrying items and for other tasks, such as winnowing seeds. The raw material to make a basket is obtained from a number of wild plants—willow, lemonadeberry, yucca, rush, tule, cottonwood, desert spoon, and beargrass, among others. But only one plant is deliberately grown for baskets: devil's claw. The black fiber stripped from the long "claw" of the dried seedpod is unmatched for durability by anything but its shorter-clawed wild relative. Devil's claw makes a wonderful garden plant for several reasons: lush foliage, fragrant snapdragon-like flowers, great tolerance for heat, and edible fruit and seeds. Of all its attributes, devil's claw is best known for the interesting dried seedpod that, while useful for basketmaking and crafts, is an admired addition to dried plant arrangements.

Devil's claw is named for its seed-dispersal strategy of hooking passing animals or people. Such a surprising ankle snag may feel as if the devil has reached up and grabbed you. Some gardeners don't like this name and prefer to call the plant unicorn plant or martynia, names used for similar wild plants found outside the Southwest. From Africa comes another plant called devil's claw, used as a medicinal herb but unrelated to our large-clawed southwestern basketry plant.

Basketmakers typically harvest the dried seedpod after the green outer husk falls away, allowing the inner woody pod to split partially in half to create the claw. Harvesters avoid the needle-sharp points during the collection process by hooking a large number of claws together, points inward, to create a wheel or ball—sometimes called a hat. Each claw can be stripped into several splints. One traditional method is to dig in with an awl where the claw meets the body of the fruit. The weaver then uses her teeth to grab a fiber splint and rotates the claw with both hands to peel the fiber slowly back all the way to the tip of the claw. Finally, the

Devil's claw is one of the strongest basketry materials available.

weaver soaks the splints in water to achieve the flexibility needed for making coiled baskets.

As one of the strongest basketry materials available, devil's claw was traditionally used to construct parts of the basket most vulnerable to wear and tear—the circular bottom or base and the outer rim. Master basketmakers can produce tightly woven, leakproof baskets with devil's claw. In fact, for a short time Native-made baskets were used as milk containers for the fledgling Arizona dairy industry. Today, when salability is more important than durability, devil's claw is primarily used to make dark designs that stand out in contrast to the lighter color of the other materials.

▲ Devil's claw seed

Wild claws have an average length of 4 to 6 inches, while the domesticated claws are 12 to 18 inches. Another telling difference: wild plants have black seeds but domesticated ones are white and therefore easier to see and collect. Domesticated claws also have a better grain; a blacker color; and more pliant, smoother, and longer fibers—all traits sought by basketmakers. As there is no evidence of improvement as a food resource (seed size, number of seeds per fruit, protein content), it is clear that it was basketmakers who brought the wild plant into their gardens and domesticated it for use as a fiber source.

The immature devil's claw fruits—both wild and garden varieties—can be cooked or pickled as an okra-like vegetable. The oil- and protein-rich kernels are a delicious, healthful snack. In some basketmaking communities there are still stories warning people not to eat the seeds—probably to protect the basketmakers' precious store of seeds. For instance, lore says that eating seeds from the occasional pod that has four claws rather than two causes the birth of twins.

The heat-loving plants need full sun. Start them indoors in short or cool-summer areas, but direct seeding is preferable in warmer areas. Pretreat the seeds before planting, as the thick seed coat will inhibit germination unless moisture gets through it to the kernel. Some gardeners scarify the seed coat, breaking through it with a file or sandpaper but not going far enough to damage the kernel. Others soak the seeds in warm water before planting (and some both scarify and soak). Carefully removing the entire seed coat, much like you would open a sunflower seed before snacking, can result in almost 100 percent germination.

Southwestern Varieties

The Tohono O'odham Domesticated will produce the long, black fibers basketmakers seek. The Domesticated Multiclawed has been selected for pods that produce three or four claws rather than the regular two. Morelos is a wild devil's claw variety, with 3- to 4-inch claws, grown for its violet flowers with a strong, beautiful fragrance.

Devil's claw bloom ▶

▲ Cotton plant

Hopi cotton seeds ▶

▼ Harvested Hopi cotton

Cotton

Of course you've worn cotton sometime this last week, but did you know that you've probably eaten some as well? While not a typical home cooking ingredient, cottonseed oil is used in a lot of snack foods (check the list of ingredients on your next bag of chips). Ground-up cottonseed meal is used as a fertilizer and is also added to some animal feeds.

Like today's commercial cotton growers, Native farmers grew this double-duty plant for both edible seeds and fiber. They roasted the seeds and ate them like peanuts. Women handspun the fibers for weavers—traditionally, Hopi weavers are older men—to use in cloth and blankets. It was an important crop in long-season areas like central Arizona, where the quantity and quality of cotton products were noted by the earliest Spanish and Anglo explorers to enter the region.

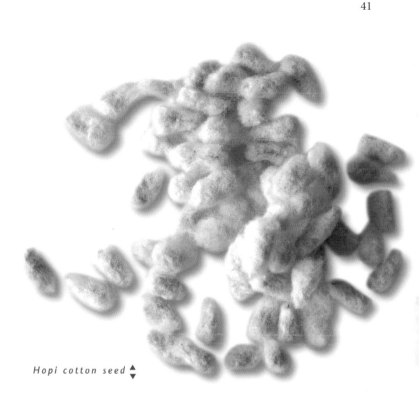

Hopi cotton seed ▲▼

Today, cotton is still an important part of Arizona's agricultural economy. Though not many people grow it as a garden crop, there is no reason not to—it's a very pretty plant. If you live in an area where cotton is grown commercially (such as the South and warmer parts of the West), you can get suggestions for planting dates, soil amendments, and how to deal with local pests from your county agricultural agent. In regions with shorter growing seasons, grow cotton in a greenhouse or in containers that can be sheltered from freezing temperatures.

◄ *Cotton flower*

▲ Gourd plants

Gourd seeds ▼

▼ Dried gourds

Gourds

Planting

Time: After the last frost

Depth: 1 inch

Space between plants: At least 1 foot, up to 8 feet between
hills of several plants

Seed preparation: Presoak or scarify seeds

Days to maturity: 110 to 180

Tips: Plants produce long climbing vines, so plant them
next to a trellis, fence, or tree.

Southwestern Native people grew hard-shelled gourds for many purposes. Durable gourds made excellent water containers essential for long-distance travel. The distinctive sound of gourd rattles and drums accompanied important ceremonies. People fashioned some gourds into face masks or used them in costumes. Other gourds became storage containers, water dippers, bowls, or other household utensils.

Worldwide, gourds come in many different sizes and shapes, but three basic types were common here: long-handled dippers, bilobed (hourglass-shaped), and canteen (round but flattened on two sides). When Apache farmers didn't have seed of the bilobed type, they tied string made from yucca plants around growing gourds to produce the hourglass or double-hourglass shape they preferred for canteens. Today, some gourd enthusiasts similarly train gourds into different shapes as they grow, even using molds to produce designs and faces.

In the backyard garden, gourd vines need a lot of space—they can grow as long as 100 feet! In large fields, gourds can be allowed to sprawl, though some sought-after gourd shapes occur only when the gourds hang freely. Gourd vines are natural climbers with strong tendrils, so most gardeners train them up trees, fences, sides of buildings, and all varieties of built trellises. Larger gourd varieties especially need sturdy trellises or arbors, and additional support (such as slings fashioned from cut-up stockings) prevents hanging gourds from breaking their vines. Techniques that keep vines and gourds off the ground also help to prevent damage from pests and disease.

▲ *Hopi Rattle gourd seed*

Gourds are best seeded directly in the ground but can be started indoors to extend growing time in short-season areas. (Plant them outside after one or two sets of true leaves have appeared.) Gourds need fertile soil and regular watering to support their prodigious growth. Some gardeners provide supplemental feeding such as fish emulsion during the growing season, but you should stop providing nitrogen fertilizer once flowers appear. Water the plants early in the day and avoid overhead sprinkling, as moisture on the leaves will promote disease. Leaves will droop during hot summer days, and if they don't revive in the evening more water is required.

The white flowers attract evening pollinators. Male blossoms appear first, growing on the main vines. Female blossoms show up several days later, growing on side branches. Female flowers are easily distinguished from male because they have a fuzzy, miniature gourd at the base of their petals. To encourage the formation of more female flowers (and thus more gourds), some gardeners nip off the tips of each primary vine, forcing branch vines to form. If female flowers aren't developing into gourds, usually due to lack of a healthy insect population, then hand-pollinate. In the early morning, use a brush to transfer pollen from several male flowers to one female. Alternatively, remove a male flower and rub it gently into a female, transferring as much pollen as possible.

Gourds take all season to fully mature. Those picked too early, or formed toward the end of the growing season, will have thin shells and will shrivel as they dry. Leave all fruit on the vine until the first good frost or until the vine has begun to die. Cut the stem several inches above the gourd and handle carefully to avoid bruises that can cause the gourd to rot. Dry the gourds in a location that allows plenty of air circulation; if possible, avoid having gourds touch each other. Depending on their size, gourds may take several weeks to almost a year to dry enough for use. When the seeds rattle when the gourd is shaken, it is fully dry.

Southwestern Varieties

Hopi Rattle gourds have the roundish, flattened shape preferred for making rattles; large ones are used to make a rasp instrument used in the home dance. O'odham Dipper gourds have handles of varying length, from 8 to 18 inches. Peyote Ceremonial gourds are small (two to four inches) bilobed gourds traditionally used by members of the Native American Church to make special rattles, and they are a perfect size for ornaments and other crafts.

▲ *Melon plant*

▼ *Tohono O'odham Yellow Meated watermelon*

Tohono O'Odham Yellow ◄
Meated watermelon seeds

Melons

Planting

Time: After the last frost

Depth: 1/2 to 1 inch

Space between plants: 3–5 plants per basin or hill, with
         basins or hills 2 feet apart

Seed preparation: None required

Days to maturity: 80 to 120

Tips: Allow ample room for vines

Juicy, sweet, and easy to grow under Southwest conditions, melons and watermelons have long been a favorite of traditional farmers. Originating in the Middle East and Africa, they were introduced to North America by the Spanish. Cultivation of melons was rapidly adopted by Native farmers, who dispersed the seed so quickly across the continent that watermelons were growing in the Southwest 100 years before the Spanish first set foot here!

Melons are tender to frost and light freezes, and require a long growing season with relatively high temperatures. Gardeners in more northerly climes start the plants indoors, place them in the sunniest spot available, and use various devices like hot caps and black plastic mulch to keep the soil and plants as warm as possible. Some newly developed varieties are better adapted to a shortened season or to greenhouse conditions.

The plants take up a lot of space and require deep soil that is well drained but has enough organic matter to retain moisture. Melons do best in soil with low levels of nitrogen and moderate amounts of potassium and phosphorus. Where spacing is a problem, train melons on a strong trellis, using netting, stockings, or strips of cloth to support the fruit. On the ground, setting fruit on empty pots, boards, or straw will prevent disease. Flowers are insect pollinated, especially by bees, and if insects are absent gardeners can hand-pollinate (see "Gourds" for details).

Melon plants are victims of many of the same pests that attack squash, such as aphids and, in the Southwest, cucumber beetles. Gardeners can deter pests using organic methods, such as spraying with soapy water and spreading diatomaceous earth. The maturing fruit attracts other hungry

> # Melons achieve full size before they are fully ripe.

pests, such as coyotes and neighbors, which gardeners can handle with strong fences and watchful eyes.

Melons achieve full size before they are fully ripe, so gardeners use a number of indicators to determine when to pick them. Watermelons are ready when (1) the tendril on the stem closest to the fruit turns brown and dry, (2) the bottom of the melon (where it touches the ground) turns from light green to creamy yellow, and (3) thumping with a knuckle produces a dull tone rather than a clear, metallic ringing tone. In addition to those rules, many melon varieties "slip" from the vine when ripe.

Hopi Yellow Meated ▼
watermelon seed

Hopi Yellow Meated ▶
watermelons

Southwestern Varieties

Among the heirloom watermelon varieties of this region, try Tohono O'odham Yellow Meated, which has crisp, sweet, yellow flesh; or Navajo Red-seeded, which has seeds redder than its flesh. Among the productive and aromatic desert-adapted melons try the delicious San Juan, a honeydew type. The casaba type O'odham Ke:li Ba:so, with tasty light green flesh, elicits giggles from Native farmers as the name describes its wrinkled skin. (Women say it means "old man's chest" and men say it means "old woman's knees.")

▲ *Sunflowers in a garden*

▼ *Tarahumara White and Hopi*
Black dried sunflower heads

Tarahumara White ◄
sunflower seeds

Sunflowers

The beauty of sunflowers has inspired artists for centuries, as shown by designs found on southwestern Native pottery, baskets, and jewelry—and by Vincent van Gogh's famous series of paintings. The large flower heads, some up to 2 feet in diameter, feature a double-spiral arrangement of seeds surrounded by showy yellow petals. Such splendor complements their usefulness to gardeners and farmers who grow sunflowers for edible seeds.

Traditional Native farmers roasted and ground sunflower seeds into meal, which they added to soups and stews or baked into cakes or bread. As they do today, children and others enjoyed cracking open the seeds and snacking on the kernels. The Hopi developed a variety with dark black seeds that make a black or purple dye for textiles, baskets, and body painting. Farmers extracted cooking and hair oil by boiling the roasted seeds and skimming oil from the surface. People also used sunflower oil

Planting

Time: After the last frost
Depth: 1 inch
Space between plants: 1 foot
Seed preparation: None required
Days to maturity: 90 to 110
Tips: Plan for tall plants.

medicinally for snakebites and wart removal. Some farmers used the dried stalks as a building material.

North American farmers domesticated the plant at least 5,000 years ago. After the first Europeans arrived, the flower was quickly adopted in Europe as an exotic garden plant. The sunflower became an important oil crop in eighteenth- and nineteenth-century Russia because the Orthodox Church did not ban its use during Advent and Lent as it did other cooking

Gardeners who want a crop must protect the flower heads.

oils. Russian varieties became the foundation for modern sunflower production. Today sunflowers are grown worldwide for oil, direct human consumption, and the growing birdseed market.

One southwestern sunflower recently made big news in Australia, where a new variety of rust, a plant fungal disease, has devastated sunflower fields. USDA research showed that a sunflower grown by the Havasupai farmers of the Grand Canyon is the only variety with genetic resistance to the disease. The Havasupai sunflower has been crossed with other sunflower varieties so that future Australian crops will naturally resist the rust, making the costly use of chemical fungicides obsolete.

Home gardeners love growing sunflowers for their beauty and edible seeds as well as to attract birds that also enjoy eating the nutritious seeds. Sunflowers are easy to grow and, thus, suitable for a child's garden. They thrive in sunny locations and can be planted strategically to shade plants on their east side. They fit in planted flowerbeds, often placed at the back so their height and showy flowers won't overwhelm the rest. When the flowers are in bud stage you will notice them tracking the sun, but once they grow larger they tend to face east all day.

Birds and other animals will swarm sunflower heads as the seeds ripen, so gardeners who want a crop must

▲ *Hopi Black Dye sunflower seed*

 protect the flower heads. Flowers can be covered with bags made from nylon stockings, cheesecloth, cotton sheeting, or any material that allows light and air to pass through (don't use plastic bags). Harvest heads when they are fully dry. Alternatively, cut off the flowers with a few inches of stalk once the seeds have full kernels (pull one out to test) and hang them in a well-ventilated area to finish drying. Extract the seeds by rubbing two dry flower heads together.

Dried sunflower seeds are a great treat raw or roasted with salt. To roast them, rinse dried seeds to remove any dirt or plant material. Soak the seeds overnight (or simmer for an hour or so) in a saltwater solution (½ cup of salt to 2 quarts water). Drain without rinsing and roast on a baking sheet in a 200°F oven for 3 hours or until crisp. Sunflower seeds are nutritional storehouses, packed with healthy fats, protein, fiber, minerals, and vitamin E.

Gardeners have many wonderful choices: The standard tall-growing sunflower with a single large head is a hit with young gardeners—look for "mammoth" or "giant" in the name. Several new types boast flowers with larger or different-colored petals, plants with multiple branches and flowers, "pollenless" varieties so that cut flowers won't cause pollen stains, or miniature plants that fit in better among other flowers.

Southwestern Varieties

Popular southwestern varieties include the Hopi Black Dye Sunflower (seeds are uniformly black) and the Tarahumara White Sunflower (with white seeds).

▲ Cilantro, tarragon, and Mexican oregano

Dried Mexican ▶
oregano

▼ Cilantro

Three Southwestern Herbs

Traditional cooks added flavor to their foods with wild plants, but once the Spanish entered the region, cultivated herbs began to influence cuisine. Some of these introduced herbs are now considered essential to regional cuisines.

Cilantro

Planting

Time: When soil temperature reaches 60 – 70°F; this cool-weather herb is a winter crop in desert areas and an early spring or late summer crop elsewhere

Depth: 1/4 to 1/2 inch

Space between plants: 4 – 6 inches

Seed preparation: Crush the capsule to release the small black seeds

Days to maturity: 70

Tips: Successive plantings every 3 to 4 weeks extend harvest time

Fresh cilantro leaves have a pungent flavor that people either strongly like or dislike. Cilantro is a common ingredient in fresh southwestern salsas and is equally delicious in soups and salads. Coriander, a spice made from the crushed seed, has a larger international appeal and has been used in medicine, cooking, and even love potions since the time of ancient Egypt.

The trick to producing cilantro is to time plantings so that you can pick leaves for a long time. Cilantro will keep growing without flowering during times of cool nights and sunny days. When the days are too hot, cilantro quickly matures, or "bolts," and the harvest ends. Cilantro is an annual, but if allowed to flower and go to seed, new plants will volunteer in the same patch next year. The delicate white flowers are also edible, and make a tasty and slightly sweet garnish. Include this pretty plant in ornamental beds.

Mexican Tarragon

Planting

Time: After the last frost, when soil temperature reaches 70°F;
   it can be started indoors 6 weeks before the last frost
Depth: 1/2 inch
Space between plants: 6 to 12 inches
Seed preparation: None required
Tips: Can be an annual or, if protected through winter, a perennial

This marigold relative has aromatic, anise-flavored leaves that are used as a tarragon substitute. Botanists know the plant as *Tagetes lucida*, but regionally it is also called Mexican Mint Marigold, Mountain Pima Anise Tea, and Texas Tarragon. Traditional cooks brew the flowers and leaves into a tea that has a mild licorice flavor and alleviates stomach ailments, colic, and malaria.

Mexican tarragon ↕

Mexican oregano ⬍

Mexican Oregano

Planting
Time: After the last frost
Depth: ¹/₂ inch
Space between plants: 6 to 12 inches
Seed preparation: None required
Tips: Can be grown in containers.

Several plant species have leaves that are grown and sold as oregano, but the southwestern variety (and, in fact, the plant that produces most of the oregano consumed in the United States) is a shrubby perennial with the scientific name *Lippia graveolens*. Its leaves are slightly bigger and stronger tasting than European oregano species. In regional cuisine, cooks often use Mexican oregano to flavor chili and bean dishes.

In cooler climates, grow Mexican oregano in a greenhouse or indoors in a container placed in a sunny, south-facing window. In warmer areas, the plant thrives in partial shade and fits in well with most ornamental plantings.

▲ Native harvest

Chiltepin pods ▼

▼ Jars of seed

▲ *Wild chiltepin seeds*

The Southwest In Your Backyard

The Companionable Three Sisters

When planted together, corn, squash, and beans are sometimes called the three sisters. Planted a week or two before the others, tall corn stalks provide a living trellis for bean vines to grow upon. Bacteria that live on the roots of bean plants turn atmospheric nitrogen into forms essential for all plants. The large leaves of sprawling squash vines create a living mulch—keeping the soil cool and moist and shading out competing weeds. These sisters really do help each other, much like human sisters often do.

With a few exceptions, southwestern Native crops are suitable for growing across the United States. Assuming your garden has fertile soil and access to sunshine, the major complicating factor might be climate. Tepary beans, for instance, will suffer from virus damage if grown where the humidity is high. Other crops—notably chiles, cotton, gourds, and melons—might need warmer temperatures or a longer growing season than occur in your region. Greenhouses, row covers, hot caps, and other devices commonly used by northern gardeners can overcome these limitations. Container growing is another option—one Boston gardener raises perennial wild chiles in pots on his balcony, bringing them inside during the winter.

Native Strategies for Pest Control

No one wants to plant a garden and have it eaten up by pests. Native farmers used all sorts of techniques to protect their harvest. They kept rodents and other animals at bay with fencing, traps, scarecrows, and by keeping pet dogs and hawks. Farmers spent time in the field to drive pests away or hunt them. A pest that becomes food is a pest no more, and in some places crafty farmers planted fake gardens to attract deer. They picked off insects by hand, cajoling them to leave by singing, praying, and talking. Some farmers used smoke to drive out particular bugs. Traditional farmers used wood ashes against corn earworms and, in an interesting biological twist, collected worms were allowed to rot in water that was then sprinkled over the field. Like other pests, Native people consumed some insects, including grasshoppers and tomato hornworms, as food.

Early histories tell us that weeds weren't much of a problem in Native fields until introduced invasive plants (such as tumbleweed, bindweed, Johnson grass, Bermuda grass, and cocklebur) entered the Southwest. Native farmers harvested some weeds for greens, including wild amaranth, lamb's-quarters, and purslane. Where water was scarce—for example in Hopi fields—farmers carefully hoed out most weeds to eliminate any competition for water.

Southwestern Water Lessons

In arid country, making the best use of water to grow food is essential for survival. In a contemporary backyard garden, water conservation means less work and lower water bills. Traditional principles can inform small-scale efforts. For instance, desert gardeners collect rainwater—much better for plants than tap water—from roofs, decks, driveways, or lawns and apply it to planting beds. They may also use sunken (rather than raised) beds to concentrate water on plants and keep young seedlings out of the hot, drying winds. To keep soils cool and conserve moisture, Pueblo farmers overtopped their fields with a layer of gravel; in your garden use mulch composed of straw, compost, or other organic material to achieve the same results.

Saving Your Own Seeds

In the past, traditional farmers saved enough seed from their crops after harvest for two years' plantings. Thus, if the next year's crop failed, they had backup seed. They stored seeds away from heat, moisture, rodents, and insects, frequently in pottery or baskets.

Seed Sources

Eastern Native Seed Conservancy
Native Seeds/SEARCH
Plants of the Southwest
Seed Savers Exchange
Seeds of Change
Southern Exposure

You can save seeds too, if you grow "open-pollinated" or heirloom varieties. Don't select from weak plants or those not true to type. Dry seeds can be frozen for 48 hours to kill any insects or insect eggs, and stored in a cool, dry location in jars, plastic bags, or coffee cans for 5 years or longer. See Suzanne Ashworth's comprehensive guide, *Seed to Seed: Seed Saving and Growing Techniques for Vegetable Gardeners* (see Further Reading) for more information.

▼ *Watermelon*

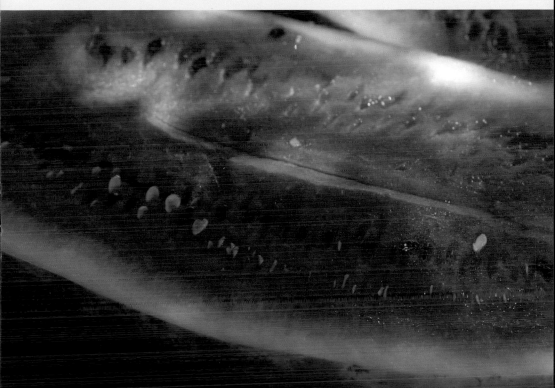

Native Seeds/SEARCH

Native Seeds/SEARCH, a nonprofit organization founded in 1983, is a conservator of Native crops of the U.S. Southwest and northwest Mexico. It promotes the use of these ancient crops by gathering, safeguarding, and distributing these seeds to the public. An integral part of the group's mission involves safeguarding 1,800 different varieties in a seed bank, returning seeds to the people who initially provided them, and supporting their traditional agricultural techniques.

Native Seeds/SEARCH operates a 60-acre farm in Patagonia, Arizona, where every year 200 to 300 different crop varieties are cultivated to produce fresh viable seed. The surplus is distributed through their seed catalog, website, and retail store located in Tucson, Arizona. To learn more about the organization visit their website at www.nativeseeds.org or call (520) 622-5561.

Further Reading

Ashworth, Suzanne. *Seed to Seed: Seed Saving and Growing Techniques for Vegetable Gardeners.* Decorah, Iowa: Seed Savers Exchange, 2002.

Bruchac, Joseph, and Michael J. Caduto. *Native American Gardening: Stories, Projects and Recipes for Families.* Golden, Colo.: Fulcrum Publishing, 1996.

Frank, Lois Ellen. *Foods of the Southwest Indian Nations.* Berkeley, Calif.: Ten Speed Press, 2004.

Hughes, Phyllis. *Pueblo Indian Cookbook: Recipes from the Pueblos of the American Southwest.* Santa Fe: Museum of New Mexico Press, 1977.

Kavena, Juanita Tiger. *Hopi Cookery.* Tucson, Ariz.: University of Arizona Press, 1980.

Nabhan, Gary Paul. *Enduring Seeds: Native American Agriculture and Wild Plant Conservation.* Tucson, Ariz.: University of Arizona Press, 2002.

Nelson, Kim. *Southwest Kitchen Garden.* Tucson, Ariz.: Rio Nuevo Publishers, 2002.

Niethammer, Carolyn. *American Indian Cooking: Recipes from the Southwest.* Lincoln, Neb.: University of Nebraska Press, 1974.

Nyhuis, Jane. *Desert Harvest: A Guide to Vegetable Gardening in Arid Lands.* Tucson, Ariz.: Growing Connections, 1995.

Owens, Dave. *Extreme Gardening: How to Grow Organic in the Hostile Deserts.* Tempe, Ariz.: Poco Verde Landscape, 2003.

Rea, Amadeo R. *At the Desert's Green Edge: An Ethnobotany of the Gila River Pima.* Tucson, Ariz.: University of Arizona Press, 1997.

Strickland, Sue. *Heirloom Vegetables: A Home Gardener's Guide to Finding and Growing Vegetables from the Past.* New York: Simon & Schuster, 1998.

Published by Western National Parks Association
The net proceeds from WNPA publications support educational and
research programs in the national parks.
Receive a free Western National Parks Association catalog featuring hundreds
of publications. Email: info@wnpa.org or visit www.wnpa.org

Written by Kevin Dahl
Edited by Abby Mogollón
Designed by Boelts/Stratford Associates
Photography by Amy Haskell
Illustrations by Boelts/Stratford Associates

The blue corn pancakes and scarlet runner bean recipes are reprinted with
permission from the book *From Furrow to Fire: Recipes from the Native
Seeds/SEARCH Community* published by Native Seed/SEARCH. Squash
blossom and roasted chile recipes are courtesy of *Hopi Cookery* by Juanita
Tiger Kavena, published by the University of Arizona Press.

Printing by Global Interprint
Printed in China

Devil's claw pod ▶